Let's Try It Out in the Air

Hands-On Early-Learning Science Activities

by **Seymour Simon** and **Nicole Fauteux**

illustrated by **Doug Cushman**

WITHDRAWN

Aladdin Paperbacks

New York   London   Toronto   Sydney   Singapore

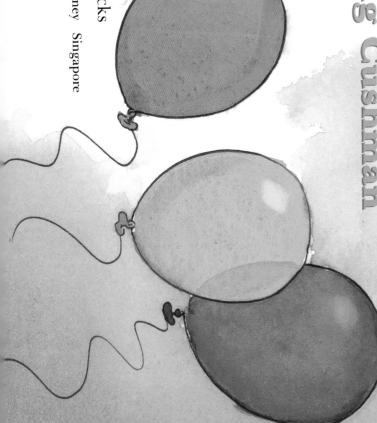

Note to Parents, Teachers, and Child-Care Providers

Let's Try It Out in the Air shows children ways that they can observe the presence of air and the pressure it exerts. Through a series of experiments and other activities derived from play, children will acquire a basic understanding of the following concepts:

- *Air moves and carries visible objects and invisible particles.*
- *Air can be captured and used to exert pressure on the inside of an object.*
- *Air can exert pressure upward and reduce the impact of gravity on an object.*
- *The effectiveness of this upward pressure increases with the surface area of an object and the movement of the air beneath it.*

The activities described in this book use these readily available materials:

- a small paper bag
- a rubber balloon*
- a piece of string
- a shoe

- a bedsheet
- several very lightweight objects
- colored paper
- liquids with distinctive odors

Feel free to make substitutions (ribbon for string, a bedspread for a sheet) and encourage the children to try the activities several times by using other materials that come to mind (kites for balloons on a string).

*Children and animals can choke on uninflated or broken balloons. Uninflated balloons should only be used with adult supervision. Discard broken balloons at once.

First Aladdin Paperbacks edition July 2003

Text copyright © 2001 by Seymour Simon and Nicole Fauteux
Illustrations copyright © by 2001 Doug Cushman

ALADDIN PAPERBACKS
An imprint of Simon & Schuster
Children's Publishing Division
1230 Avenue of the Americas
New York, NY 10020

Also available in a Simon & Schuster Books for Young Readers hardcover edition.
Designed by Anahid Hamparian

The text of this book was set in 19-point New Baskerville.

Manufactured in China
2 4 6 8 10 9 7 5 3 1

The Library of Congress has cataloged the hardcover edition as follows:
Simon, Seymour.
Let's try it out in the air / by Seymour Simon and Nicole Fauteux.
p. cm.

Summary: Presents simple activities and experiments that demonstrate the properties of air by observing the presence of air and the pressure it exerts.

1. Air—Juvenile literature. [1. Air experiments. 2. Experiments.] I. Fauteux, Nicole. II. Title
ISBN 0-689-82918-3 (hc.)
QC161.2.S56 2000   99-20370
532'.6—dc21   CIP
ISBN 0-689-86011-0 (pbk.)

To Nicole and Robert, Debra and Michael, and their wonderful kids:
Joel and Benjamin, Chloe and Jeremy —S. S.

To Bob, Joel, and Benjamin, with love

Thanks to Martha Hummer and her morning kindergartners at Olde Creek
Elementary School for trying these activities out. —N. F.

Imagine that you are outside on a windy day.
Do you feel the wind pushing against your face? Do you
see the wind blowing through your friend's hair?

Wind is air that moves. You can't see moving air, but you can feel it pushing against you.

How do you know that the air is **still** there when it's not moving? Is there a way you can trap the air?

Let's try it out.

Open your mouth. Breathe deeply, in and out. Can you feel the air moving over your lips?

Take a deep breath and hold it. Your lungs fill with air. Can you feel your chest puff up?

What else can you fill with air? A paper bag? A balloon?

Let's try it out.

Hold a small paper bag in front of your mouth and blow into it. Blow hard.

What happens when you blow the air from your lungs into the bag? Does the bag rise and fall as you breathe in and out? Is the bag getting bigger?

Imagine you and your friends are very tiny. One by one you crawl inside the paper bag. You try to stand up, but the bag lies flat on your backs like a blanket. What can you do to make a big space inside the bag so everyone can stand?

Did you think about pushing against the walls of the bag? When you blow air into the bag, that is what the air does. It pushes against the paper and puffs up the bag.

Hold an empty balloon in your hands. Without air inside, is the balloon big or small, round or flat, stiff or floppy? What happens when you fill a balloon with air?

Let's try it out.

Ask a grown-up to blow air into a balloon and knot the end. How has the balloon changed? What is the air doing to the balloon?

You can use a balloon to play volleyball with your friends. If you tap it upward, it will stay in the air long enough for one of your friends to tap it back to you.

The balloon is so light that it can float, or rest, on the air. But without your taps it won't stay up for very long. When you stop playing, the balloon falls to the floor.

Take the balloon outside on a windy day. Let go of the balloon and . . . the moving air snatches it away from you. You try to catch it, but you can't keep up. The wind makes the balloon fly up and down, like a stunt plane out of control.

Can you make your balloon fly?

Let's try it out.

Tie a string or a ribbon to your balloon. Hold the string in your hand and run. Twirl the balloon around and around.

When you move, the balloon is held up by the air. Does the balloon stay up when you stand still? What happens to the balloon when you move slowly? What happens when you run fast?

Even heavy objects can be held up by the air when it moves rapidly. An airplane is much heavier than a balloon, but when a propeller or a jet engine makes a plane move through the air fast enough, the air pushes up against the wings of the plane and holds it up in the sky.

How long can you a keep a balloon in the air by moving the air beneath it?

Let's try it out.

Stand facing a friend who is about your height. Hold a balloon up high between the two of you. Count to three, take a deep breath, then let go of the balloon and blow. See how long you and your friend can keep the balloon up by blowing. Challenge two more friends to a contest and see who can keep the balloon up longest.

Pick up a shoe and drop it in midair. What happens? You are strong enough to hold your shoe up off the floor, but the air is not.

If something is light enough, even air that is moving slowly can hold it up.

Now look around for some lighter things like a feather, a scarf, or a paper airplane. Do you think these things will fall to the floor as quickly as the shoe, or will they float in the air for a moment before reaching the ground?

Let's try it out.

Hold the shoe and one of the lighter things you found straight out in front of you. Now let go. What reaches the ground first?

Try the same experiment with the other things you found. Do they fall straight down, or do some of them float on their way to the floor?

Try throwing the paper airplane. How long can it glide in the air before it falls to the ground?

Lightweight things float because the air is holding them up in much the same way that water holds up a floating object.

The air doesn't press hard enough to hold up a shoe, but it is strong enough to hold up some tiny things for a very long time.

Stand near a window on a day when bright sunlight is streaming in. Look at the rays of sunlight inside the room. Do you see something floating in the air?

Tiny specks of dust float in the air around us. They are so small that they are almost invisible. You can only see them in a shaft of sunlight in a darkened room.

After a while the dust specks will fall to the floor like your shoe did, but first you can watch them float for a very long time.

Dust specks are not the only tiny things floating in the air. Smells float, too.

Walk toward the kitchen just before dinnertime, or toward the school cafeteria before lunch. Do you smell pizza or hot dogs or beans? Can you tell what the meal will be before you see it? Where do you first smell the food? In the hallway? At the door?

You won't know for sure how the food tastes until it touches your tongue, but your nose can make a pretty good guess from many feet away.

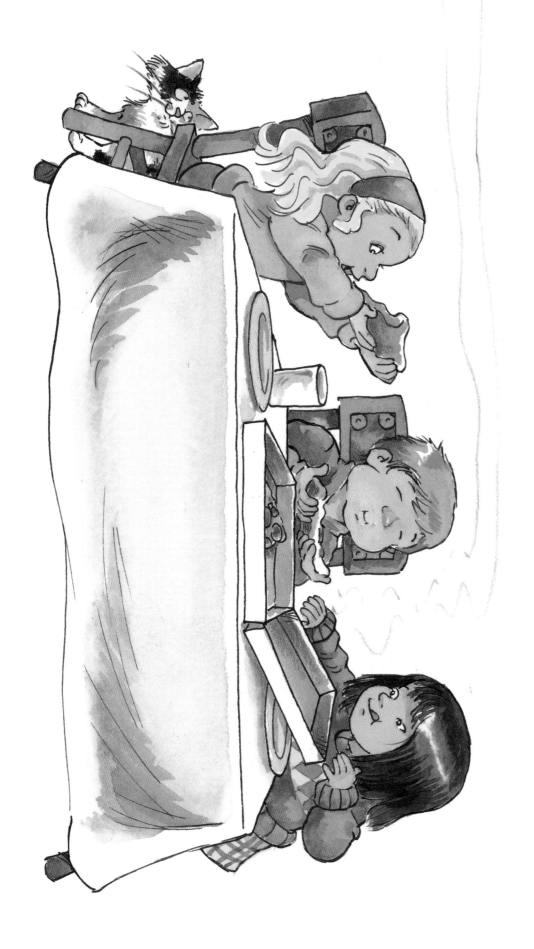

Try the same thing outside your home or school.

Do you smell the stink when a garbage truck passes? Do you smell cookies from a bakery nearby? Do you smell the salt air of an ocean breeze? Does flower pollen make you sneeze?

You can't see smells, but very tiny bits of food and salt and smoke ride in the air and reach your nose.

P.U.! Yum! At-choo!

Imagine you are on a camping trip. You unpack your gear and discover that you have forgotten the poles for your tent. Can you use air to hold it up?

Find a bedsheet, the bigger the better. Spread it flat on the ground. Then ask a few of your friends to help you by picking up a corner or a side.

Tell everyone to throw the sheet up into the air, but don't let go! When the sheet is over your heads, sit down under it as fast as all of you can.

What is holding up your tent? You guessed it: the air.

Now that you know how how the air can push and carry, you can put on an "air show" for your friends and family.

Make a squadron of balloons or kites soar through the sky, loop around, and do figure eights.

Choose someone from your audience to help you suspend a balloon in midair and then wow the crowd.

Tell them you are so good at identifying different-colored paper airplanes that you can do it blindfolded. (Here's the trick: Put a few drops of different-smelling liquids, like perfume or lemon juice or coffee on each plane before the show. Then ask someone from the audience to choose a plane and hand it to you. You will know which one it is by the smell.)

For a fun finale, invite everyone to help you pitch a tent.

Your show will be air-resistible.

Let's Try It Out in the Air is structured so that teachers can present all the activities in a single session. With younger children, teachers may prefer to cover the material in two or three twenty- to thirty-minute sessions over the course of a week. Ideally, the class should be divided into smaller groups so that each child can fully experience each of the activities for himself or herself.

Parents and caregivers may find it more rewarding to use the book in shorter time intervals, pulling it off the shelf to introduce an activity when they find their children already engaged in related play. When balloons are present at a party, children can be asked to make them "fly," or invited to play balloon volleyball. Before lunches are packed, children can be asked to blow up the paper bags. What is in the bag? Where did it come from? What is the air doing to the bag?

The *Let's Try It Out* series integrates the scientific method into everyday life by using only safe, readily available materials and by modeling the experiments it presents on play. The books encourage children to use their body and their senses to explore their surroundings.

Parents and teachers can use these books to help children make observations in the course of their play, recognize the significance of these observations, and organize them in such a way that children can draw some preliminary conclusions about how things work in the fascinating world around them.

Parents and teachers should not be disturbed if children sometimes draw the wrong conclusions from these activities. Children's cognitive development varies greatly at young ages, and some children may not yet be able to grasp every concept presented. Forcing children to accept your explanation of a phenomenon they cannot understand will undermine your main goals of teaching them to observe carefully, form hypotheses, and test them. Chances are that if you reintroduce a challenging activity six months later, a child will be ready to draw the right conclusion for himself or herself.

You can also use the Internet to find out more about this book and others in the series. Visit our Web site at www.SimonSaysKids.com. We value your suggestions and comments about your experiences using our books with your children.

Seymour Simon
Nicole Fauteux